5 Ingredient Dinner Recipes

Hannah Abedi

Introduction

Here it is! A cookbook of 100 recipes that contain FIVE ingredients or less! Save money and time with these simple to follow and cook recipes. And there are actually ONLY five (or less) ingredients in each recipe, with the exception of salt and pepper in a few recipes.

I'm not very fond of recipes that claim to be five ingredient recipes but then contain a bunch of ingredients that are assumed to be "staples" that you should already have in your kitchen! While I'm sure many of you have a basic foundation of spices and oils in your cabinet, I did not depend on that for these recipes. I hope you enjoy this book and get as much joy from cooking and eating the foods in it as I have gotten from creating it for you.

Abbreviations & Conversions

Abbreviations

oz = ounce
fl oz = fluid ounce
tsp = teaspoon
tbsp = tablespoon
ml = milliliter

c = cup
pt = pint
qt = quart
gal = gallon
L = liter

Kitchen Conversions

1/2 fl oz = 3 tsp = 1 tbsp = 15 ml
1 fl oz = 2 tbsp = 1/8 c = 30 ml
2 fl oz = 4 tbsp = 1/4 c = 60 ml
4 fl oz = 8 tbsp = 1/2 c = 118 ml
8 fl oz = 16 tbsp = 1 c = 236 ml
16 fl oz = 1 pt = 1/2 qt = 2 c = 473 ml
128 fl oz = 8 pt = 4 qt = 1 gal = 3.78 L

My Free Gift

www.makingofmama.com/freegift

Do you want to know how I made 26 freezer meals for $119 in 5 hours? Instantly download my free eBook that explains the entire process from start to finish. Everything is explained in simple and easy, step-by-step instructions. Enjoy!

CONTENTS

CHICKEN RECIPES

Asian Chicken

Servings: 4

Ingredients:

- 4 chicken breasts
- 1/4 cup sesame oil
- 2 tbsp seasoned rice vinegar
- 2 tsp soy sauce

Directions:

1. Place all of the ingredients into a gallon ziplock bag and toss to coat the chicken well.
2. Place the bag in the refrigerator and let it sit for 2-8 hours.
3. Heat a skillet over medium-high heat.
4. Place the chicken in the heated skillet and cook on each side for 3-5 minutes or until the inside is completely cooked.

Tex-Mex Chicken

Servings: 4

Ingredients:

- 4 chicken breasts
- 1/4 cup canola oil
- 2 tbsp lime juice
- 2 tsp taco seasoning

Directions:

1. Place all of the ingredients into a gallon ziplock bag and toss to coat the chicken well.
2. Place the bag in the refrigerator and let it sit for 2-8 hours.
3. Heat a skillet over medium-high heat.
4. Place the chicken in the heated skillet and cook on each side for 3-5 minutes or until the inside is completely cooked.

Yellow Chicken

Servings: 4

Ingredients:

- 4 chicken breasts
- 1/4 cup canola oil
- 2 tbsp lemon juice
- 1 tsp turmeric powder

Directions:

1. Place all of the ingredients into a gallon ziplock bag and toss to coat the chicken well.
2. Place the bag in the refrigerator and let it sit for 2-8 hours.
3. Heat a skillet over medium-high heat.
4. Place the chicken in the heated skillet and cook on each side for 3-5 minutes or until the inside is completely cooked.

Slow Cooker Russian Chicken

Servings: 4

Ingredients:

- 1 12-oz jar of apricot preserves
- 1 12-oz bottle of Russian salad dressing
- 2 lbs boneless, skinless chicken breasts
- 1 small onion, chopped

Directions:

1. Add all of the ingredients to your slow cooker.
2. Stir together.
3. Cook on low for 8 hours.
4. Serve with rice or mashed potatoes.

Ranch Chicken

Servings: 4

Ingredients:

- 4 chicken breasts
- 1/4 cup canola oil
- 1/4 cup buttermilk
- 1 tbsp ranch seasoning

Directions:

1. Place all of the ingredients into a gallon ziplock bag and toss to coat the chicken well.
2. Place the bag in the refrigerator and let it sit for 2-8 hours.
3. Heat a skillet over medium-high heat.
4. Place the chicken in the heated skillet and cook on each side for 3-5 minutes or until the inside is completely cooked.

Old Bay Chicken

Servings: 4

Ingredients:

- 4 chicken breasts
- 1/4 cup canola oil
- 2 tbsp buttermilk
- 2 tsp Old Bay seasoning

Directions:

1. Place all of the ingredients into a gallon ziplock bag and toss to coat the chicken well.
2. Place the bag in the refrigerator and let it sit for 2-8 hours.
3. Heat a skillet over medium-high heat.
4. Place the chicken in the heated skillet and cook on each side for 3-5 minutes or until the inside is completely cooked.

Worcestershire Chicken

Servings: 4

Ingredients:

- 4 chicken breasts
- 1/4 cup peanut oil
- 2 tbsp apple cider vinegar
- 2 tsp Worcestershire sauce

Directions:

1. Place all of the ingredients into a gallon ziplock bag and toss to coat the chicken well.
2. Place the bag in the refrigerator and let it sit for 2-8 hours.
3. Heat a skillet over medium-high heat.
4. Place the chicken in the heated skillet and cook on each side for 3-5 minutes or until the inside is completely cooked.

Slow Cooker Buffalo Chicken

Servings: 4

Ingredients:

- 4 chicken breasts
- 12 oz bottle of buffalo wing sauce
- 2 tbsp ranch mix
- 2 tbsp butter
- 2 cloves garlic, minced

Directions:

1. Place the chicken breasts in a slow cooker.
2. Pour the wing sauce over the chicken.
3. Sprinkle ranch mix over the sauce.
4. Add butter and garlic to the slow cooker.
5. Cook on low for 4-6 hours or until chicken shreds easily.
6. Remove chicken from the slow cooker and shred it completely.
7. Put the shredded chicken back into the slow cooker and cook on low for another hour before serving.

Island Chicken

Servings: 4

Ingredients:

- 4 chicken breasts
- 1/4 cup canola oil
- 2 tbsp pineapple juice
- 1 tsp salt

Directions:

1. Place all of the ingredients into a gallon ziplock bag and toss to coat the chicken well.
2. Place the bag in the refrigerator and let it sit for 2-8 hours.
3. Heat a skillet over medium-high heat.
4. Place the chicken in the heated skillet and cook on each side for 3-5 minutes or until the inside is completely cooked.

Miso Chicken

Servings: 4

Ingredients:

- 4 chicken breasts
- 1/4 cup sesame oil
- 2 tbsp rice vinegar
- 1 tsp miso

Directions:

1. Place all of the ingredients into a gallon ziplock bag and toss to coat the chicken well.
2. Place the bag in the refrigerator and let it sit for 2-8 hours.
3. Heat a skillet over medium-high heat.
4. Place the chicken in the heated skillet and cook on each side for 3-5 minutes or until the inside is completely cooked.

Slow Cooker Mexican Chicken

Servings: 4

Ingredients:

- 4 chicken breasts
- 1 tbsp taco seasoning
- 1/2 cup enchilada sauce
- 1 cup shredded cheddar cheese
- 3 green onions, chopped

Directions:

1. Add the chicken, taco seasoning, and enchilada sauce to a slow cooker and cook on low for 4-6 hours.
2. Shred chicken with a fork.
3. Stir in cheese and cook for another hour.
4. Stir in green onions before serving.

Hawaiian Chicken

Servings: 4

Ingredients:

- 4 chicken breasts
- 1/4 cup coconut milk
- 2 tbsp pineapple juice
- 2 tsp fish sauce

Directions:

1. Place all of the ingredients into a gallon ziplock bag and toss to coat the chicken well.
2. Place the bag in the refrigerator and let it sit for 2-8 hours.
3. Heat a skillet over medium-high heat.
4. Place the chicken in the heated skillet and cook on each side for 3-5 minutes or until the inside is completely cooked.

Sriracha Chicken

Servings: 4

Ingredients:

- 4 chicken breasts
- 1/4 cup canola oil
- 2 tbsp seasoned rice vinegar
- 2 tsp Sriracha
- 2 tsp honey

Directions:

1. Place all of the ingredients into a gallon ziplock bag and toss to coat the chicken well.
2. Place the bag in the refrigerator and let it sit for 2-8 hours.
3. Heat a skillet over medium-high heat.
4. Place the chicken in the heated skillet and cook on each side for 3-5 minutes or until the inside is completely cooked.

Greek Chicken

Servings: 4

Ingredients:

- 4 chicken breasts
- 1/4 cup peanut oil
- 2 tbsp plain Greek yogurt
- 1 tsp salt
- 2 tsp cumin

Directions:

1. Place all of the ingredients into a gallon ziplock bag and toss to coat the chicken well.
2. Place the bag in the refrigerator and let it sit for 2-8 hours.
3. Heat a skillet over medium-high heat.
4. Place the chicken in the heated skillet and cook on each side for 3-5 minutes or until the inside is completely cooked.

Balsamic Chicken

Servings: 4

Ingredients:

- 4 chicken breasts
- 1/4 cup extra virgin olive oil
- 2 tbsp balsamic vinegar
- 1 tsp salt
- 2 tsp chopped garlic

Directions:

1. Place all of the ingredients into a gallon ziplock bag and toss to coat the chicken well.
2. Place the bag in the refrigerator and let it sit for 2-8 hours.
3. Heat a skillet over medium-high heat.
4. Place the chicken in the heated skillet and cook on each side for 3-5 minutes or until the inside is completely cooked.

Buffalo Chicken Sliders

Servings: 6-8

Ingredients:

- 3 chicken breasts
- 1 12-oz bottle of buffalo wing sauce, divided
- 1 package of ranch seasoning mix
- 2 tbsp butter
- 2 packs of Hawaiian rolls

Directions:

1. Place the chicken breasts into your slow cooker and pour in ¾ of the wing sauce and all of the ranch seasoning mix. Cover and cook for 6-7 hours or until the chicken easily shreds.
2. Once the chicken is cooked, drain off the liquid.
3. Add the butter, the rest of the buffalo sauce, and shred the chicken with two forks.
4. Spoon the shredded chicken onto Hawaiian rolls and serve.

Rosemary Orange Chicken

Servings: 4

Ingredients:

- 4 chicken breasts
- 1/4 cup canola oil
- 2 tbsp orange juice
- 1 tsp salt
- 2 tsp chopped rosemary

Directions:

1. Place all of the ingredients into a gallon ziplock bag and toss to coat the chicken well.
2. Place the bag in the refrigerator and let it sit for 2-8 hours.
3. Heat a skillet over medium-high heat.
4. Place the chicken in the heated skillet and cook on each side for 3-5 minutes or until the inside is completely cooked.

Garlic Chicken

Servings: 4

Ingredients:

- 4 chicken breasts
- 1/4 cup canola oil
- 2 tbsp minced garlic
- 1 tsp salt

Directions:

1. Place all of the ingredients into a gallon ziplock bag and toss to coat the chicken well.
2. Place the bag in the refrigerator and let it sit for 2-8 hours.
3. Heat a skillet over medium-high heat.
4. Place the chicken in the heated skillet and cook on each side for 3-5 minutes or until the inside is completely cooked.

Coconut Chicken

Servings: 4

Ingredients:

- 4 chicken breasts
- 1/4 cup coconut milk
- 2 tbsp lemon juice
- 1 tsp salt

Directions:

1. Place all of the ingredients into a gallon ziplock bag and toss to coat the chicken well.
2. Place the bag in the refrigerator and let it sit for 2-8 hours.
3. Heat a skillet over medium-high heat.
4. Place the chicken in the heated skillet and cook on each side for 3-5 minutes or until the inside is completely cooked.

SoCo Chicken

Servings: 4

Ingredients:

- 4 chicken breasts
- 1/4 cup canola oil
- 2 tbsp lime juice
- 1 tsp salt
- 2 tsp Southern Comfort

Directions:

1. Place all of the ingredients into a gallon ziplock bag and toss to coat the chicken well.
2. Place the bag in the refrigerator and let it sit for 2-8 hours.
3. Heat a skillet over medium-high heat.
4. Place the chicken in the heated skillet and cook on each side for 3-5 minutes or until the inside is completely cooked.

Sweet Heat Chicken

Servings: 4

Ingredients:

- 4 chicken breasts
- 1/4 cup canola oil
- 2 tbsp lemon juice
- 1 tsp cayenne pepper
- 2 tsp maple syrup

Directions:

1. Place all of the ingredients into a gallon ziplock bag and toss to coat the chicken well.
2. Place the bag in the refrigerator and let it sit for 2-8 hours.
3. Heat a skillet over medium-high heat.
4. Place the chicken in the heated skillet and cook on each side for 3-5 minutes or until the inside is completely cooked.

Tabasco Chicken

Servings: 4

Ingredients:

- 4 chicken breasts
- 1/4 cup peanut oil
- 2 tbsp buttermilk
- 2 tsp tabasco
- 2 tsp chopped garlic

Directions:

1. Place all of the ingredients into a gallon ziplock bag and toss to coat the chicken well.
2. Place the bag in the refrigerator and let it sit for 2-8 hours.
3. Heat a skillet over medium-high heat.
4. Place the chicken in the heated skillet and cook on each side for 3-5 minutes or until the inside is completely cooked.

Ginger Chicken

Servings: 4

Ingredients:

- 4 chicken breasts
- 1/4 cup sesame oil
- 2 tbsp rice vinegar
- 1 tsp fish sauce
- 2 tsp chopped ginger

Directions:

1. Place all of the ingredients into a gallon ziplock bag and toss to coat the chicken well.
2. Place the bag in the refrigerator and let it sit for 2-8 hours.
3. Heat a skillet over medium-high heat.
4. Place the chicken in the heated skillet and cook on each side for 3-5 minutes or until the inside is completely cooked.

Soy Sweet Chicken

Servings: 4

Ingredients:

- 4 chicken breasts
- 1/4 cup canola oil
- 2 tbsp orange juice
- 2 tsp soy sauce
- 2 tsp sugar

Directions:

1. Place all of the ingredients into a gallon ziplock bag and toss to coat the chicken well.
2. Place the bag in the refrigerator and let it sit for 2-8 hours.
3. Heat a skillet over medium-high heat.
4. Place the chicken in the heated skillet and cook on each side for 3-5 minutes or until the inside is completely cooked.

Sweet Miso Chicken

Servings: 4

Ingredients:

- 4 chicken breasts
- 1/4 cup canola oil
- 2 tbsp lemon juice
- 2 tsp miso
- 2 tsp honey

Directions:

1. Place all of the ingredients into a gallon ziplock bag and toss to coat the chicken well.
2. Place the bag in the refrigerator and let it sit for 2-8 hours.
3. Heat a skillet over medium-high heat.
4. Place the chicken in the heated skillet and cook on each side for 3-5 minutes or until the inside is completely cooked.

Sriracha Lime Chicken

Servings: 4

Ingredients:

- 4 chicken breasts
- 1/4 cup sesame oil
- 2 tbsp lime juice
- 2 tsp Sriracha
- 2 tsp sugar

Directions:

1. Place all of the ingredients into a gallon ziplock bag and toss to coat the chicken well.
2. Place the bag in the refrigerator and let it sit for 2-8 hours.
3. Heat a skillet over medium-high heat.
4. Place the chicken in the heated skillet and cook on each side for 3-5 minutes or until the inside is completely cooked.

Slow Cooker Teriyaki Chicken

Servings: 4

Ingredients:

- 4 boneless skinless chicken breasts
- 1 tsp minced garlic
- 1/2 cup soy sauce
- 2 tbsp brown sugar
- 2 tbsp rice vinegar

Directions:

1. Place all of the ingredients into your slow cooker and cook on high for 4 hours or low for 8 hours.

Cumin Turmeric Chicken

Servings: 4

Ingredients:

- 4 chicken breasts
- 1/4 cup canola oil
- 2 tbsp lemon juice
- 1 tsp turmeric powder
- 2 tsp cumin

Directions:

1. Place all of the ingredients into a gallon ziplock bag and toss to coat the chicken well.
2. Place the bag in the refrigerator and let it sit for 2-8 hours.
3. Heat a skillet over medium-high heat.
4. Place the chicken in the heated skillet and cook on each side for 3-5 minutes or until the inside is completely cooked.

Honey Chicken

Servings: 4

Ingredients:

- 4 chicken breasts
- 1/3 cup melted butter
- 1/3 cup honey
- 2 tbsp spicy brown mustard
- 1/4 tsp salt

Directions:

1. Preheat your oven to 350 degrees F.
2. Place the chicken breasts in a shallow square baking pan.
3. Combine the butter, honey, mustard, and salt in a small bowl. Pour this mixture over the chicken.
4. Bake for 1 hour or to a minimal internal temperature of 165 degrees F. Baste every 15 minutes while baking.

Maple Mustard Baked Chicken

Servings: 4

Ingredients:

- 4 chicken breasts
- 1/2 cup spicy brown mustard
- 1/4 cup maple syrup
- 1 tbsp red wine vinegar
- Salt and pepper, to taste

Directions:

1. Preheat your oven to 425 degrees F.
2. In a medium sized bowl, mix together the mustard, syrup, and vinegar.
3. Place the chicken into a 9x13 baking dish and season with salt and pepper.
4. Pour the mustard mixture over the chicken.
5. Bake for 30-40 minutes or until the internal temperature of the chicken reaches 165 degrees F.

Easy Italian Baked Chicken

Servings: 4

Ingredients:

- 4 chicken breasts
- 1 packet dry Italian dressing mix
- 1/2 cup packed brown sugar

Directions:

1. Preheat your oven to 350 degrees and line a 9x13 baking dish with aluminum foil.
2. In a small bowl, mix together the Italian dressing mix and the brown sugar.
3. Place the chicken breasts between two sheets of wax or parchment paper and pound them until they are thin.
4. Cut each chicken breast in half.
5. Dip each piece of chicken into the Italian dressing/sugar mixture and coat well.
6. Place the chicken into the baking pan.
7. Sprinkle any remaining seasoning mixture onto the chicken.
8. Bake for 20-30 minutes or until the internal temp is 165 degrees F. Flip the chicken over after about 15 minutes.
9. Broil the chicken on each side for 1-2 minutes before removing from the oven.

Chicken and Cheese Rolls

Servings:

Ingredients:

- 1 package 6-count refrigerated crescent rolls
- 2 cups chopped cooked chicken
- 2 cups shredded cheddar cheese
- 1 10.75-oz can of cream of chicken soup
- 1 cup of milk

Directions:

1. Preheat your oven to 350 degrees F and spray a baking dish with non-stick spray.
2. Separate the crescent rolls and unroll them onto a clean surface.
3. In a medium bowl, mix together the cream of chicken soup and milk.
4. Place a spoonful of chicken and a spoonful of cheese on the large part of each crescent roll.
5. Roll each crescent roll up and pinch the seal together.
6. Place each roll in the prepared baking dish.
7. Pour the soup mixture over the rolls.
8. Bake for 30 minutes.

Slow Cooker Cranberry Orange Chicken

Servings: 4

Ingredients:

- 4 boneless, skinless chicken breasts
- 1/4 cup orange juice
- 1/2 cup cranberry juice
- 2 tbsp butter, melted
- 1 tbsp soy sauce

Directions:

1. Add all of the ingredients to your slow cooker.
2. Stir together.
3. Cook on low for 8 hours.

Slow Cooker Dijon Lime Chicken

Servings: 4

Ingredients:

- 4 boneless, skinless chicken breasts
- 2 tsp minced garlic
- 4 tbsp Dijon mustard
- 2 tbsp lime juice

Directions:

1. Add all of the ingredients to your slow cooker.
2. Stir together.
3. Cook on low for 8 hours.

Lemon Pepper Chicken

Servings: 4

Ingredients:

- 1 lb boneless skinless chicken breasts
- 1/4 cup flour
- 1/2 tsp salt
- 2 tbsp butter
- 1 tsp lemon pepper seasoning

Directions:

1. Pound the chicken breasts until they are about 1/2 inch thick each.
2. Place the flour and salt in a shallow dish and toss each breast in it.
3. Melt the butter in a large skillet over medium heat.
4. Cook the chicken for 4 minutes on each side or until golden brown.
5. Sprinkle each side of the chicken with lemon pepper seasoning.

Chicken Burritos

Servings: 4

Ingredients:

- Package of 8 flour tortillas, burrito size
- 1 can of enchilada sauce
- 2 cups shredded cooked chicken
- 1 red bell pepper, sliced thin
- Shredded cheese

Directions:

1. Preheat your oven to 400 degrees F.
2. Pour 1/4 of the enchilada sauce into the bottom of a 9x13 inch pan.
3. Divide the chicken and sliced bell peppers evenly between the 8 tortillas and add a couple tablespoons of cheese and enchilada sauce to each tortilla.
4. Roll up each tortilla and place seam side down into the prepared pan.
5. Pour the rest of the enchilada sauce over the burritos and top with a cup of cheese (more or less if you like).
6. Bake for 20 minutes or until cheese is and sauce are bubbly.

Brown Sugar Italian Chicken

Servings: 4

Ingredients:

- 4 boneless, skinless chicken breasts
- 1/2 cup brown sugar
- 1 0.7-oz package of Italian dressing mix

Directions:

1. Preheat your oven to 425 degrees F and line a baking pan with foil.
2. In a small bowl, stir together the brown sugar and the Italian dressing mix.
3. Coat both sides of the chicken with the mixture.
4. Place the chicken on the prepared pan and sprinkle the remaining mixture over the chicken.
5. Bake for 20 minutes.
6. Turn the broiler on high and cook for 2 minutes or until the brown sugar caramelizes.

Chicken Tortilla Bake

Servings: 8

Ingredients:

- 2 10-oz cans cream of chicken soup
- 1 10-oz can of diced tomatoes with green chiles
- 12 6-inch corn tortillas, cut into small strips
- 3 cups cooked shredded chicken
- 2 cups shredded taco blend cheese

Directions:

1. Preheat your oven to 350 degrees F. Grease a 9x13-inch casserole dish with nonstick spray.
2. In a medium bowl, stir together the tomatoes, cream of chicken soup mix, and 1 cup of cheese.
3. Layer one third of the tortilla strips over the bottom of the casserole dish. Layer half of the chicken over the tortillas. Spoon half of the spoon mixture over the chicken.
4. Repeat layers.
5. Cover with foil and bake for 40 minutes or until bubbly and hot.
6. Uncover and sprinkle on the rest of the cheese and bake for another 5 minutes.

Slow Cooker Butter Ranch Chicken

Servings: 4

Ingredients:

- 4 chicken breasts
- 1 packet of ranch seasoning
- 1 stick of butter

Directions:

1. Place the chicken into your slow cooker.
2. Sprinkle the ranch mix over the chicken.
3. Slice the butter and place the slices on the chicken.
4. Cook on low for 6-8 hours.

Breaded Lemon Chicken

Servings: 4

Ingredients:

- 4 chicken breasts
- 1/2 cup lemon juice
- 1 1/2 cups seasoned bread crumbs
- Vegetable oil, for frying
- Lemon pepper, to taste

Directions:

1. Pound the breasts out until they are 1/4" thin.
2. Pour the lemon juice in a large shallow dish. Place the chicken breasts in the lemon juice and cover. Refrigerate for at least 1 hour.
3. Heat 1/4" of vegetable oil in a large pan over medium heat.
4. Put the breadcrumbs in a shallow bowl.
5. After the chicken has soaked in the lemon juice, dredge each piece in the breadcrumbs until they are well covered.
6. Add the chicken, 2 at a time, to the heated oil. Sprinkle with lemon pepper.
7. Cook for 4 minutes, turn over with tongs, and sprinkle the other side with lemon pepper.
8. Cook for another 4 minutes. Remove from the oil and place on a paper towel lined plate.

Roasted Chicken and Veggies

Servings: 4

Ingredients:

- 4 boneless chicken breasts
- 4 large carrots, peeled and chopped
- 1 lb new potatoes, sliced in half
- 1/4 cup balsamic vinaigrette
- 2 tbsp grated parmesan cheese

Directions:

1. Preheat your oven to 400 degrees F. Line a baking sheet with foil.
2. Place the carrots and potatoes into a large bowl and toss with half of the balsamic vinaigrette.
3. Spread the vegetables on the baking sheet.
4. Toss the chicken with the remaining dressing and place on the baking sheet with the vegetables.
5. Bake for 40 minutes or until the chicken is done. Turn the vegetables after 20 minutes.
6. Before serving, sprinkle with cheese.

Asian Grilled Chicken Thighs

Servings: 2

Ingredients:

- 4 chicken thighs
- 2 tbsp sesame seeds
- 1 tbsp sesame oil
- 1/4 cup soy sauce
- 2 tbsp tomato paste

Directions:

1. Preheat your grill to 400 degrees. You could also do this in the oven at the same temperature.
2. In a mixing bowl, stir together the tomato paste, sesame seeds, sesame oil, and soy sauce.
3. Coat the chicken with the sauce and place them on the grill.
4. Bake for 20-25 minutes or until the chicken is done.

Chipotle Chicken Kabobs

Servings: 4

Ingredients:

- 1 1/2 lbs boneless skinless chicken breasts
- 8 strips of bacon
- 1 cup barbeque sauce
- 2 chipotle peppers in adobo sauce

Directions:

1. Soak 8 wooden skewers in water for 30 minutes.
2. Preheat your grill to medium.
3. Cut the chicken breasts into 3/4-inch pieces.
4. Cut the bacon into 3/4-inch pieces
5. Alternate threading the chicken and bacon onto the skewers.
6. Puree the barbeque sauce and chipotle peppers in adobo sauce until smooth.
7. Grill the kabobs for 4 minutes on each side then brush with the sauce and grill for another 3 minutes on each side or until bacon is crisp.

Honey Garlic Chicken Wings

Servings: 4

Ingredients:

- 2 lbs chicken wings
- 1 cup honey
- 1/4 cup soy sauce
- 3 cloves garlic, minced

Directions:

1. In a small bowl, stir together the honey, soy sauce, and garlic.
2. Put the chicken in a baking dish and pour the sauce over it. Cover and refrigerate for several hours or overnight.
3. Preheat your oven to 375 degrees F.
4. Cover the baking dish and bake for 1 hour. Turn the wings over after 30 minutes.
5. Bake uncovered for 20 minutes. Turn the wings over after 10 minutes.

Honey Ginger Chicken

Servings: 6

Ingredients:

- 3 lbs boneless chicken thighs
- 1 cup honey, divided
- 3/4 cup soy sauce
- 8 cloves garlic, minced
- 1/4 cup peeled and grated ginger root

Directions:

1. Preheat your oven to 375 degrees F and line a baking sheet with foil.
2. Mix 3/4 cup honey, soy sauce, ginger, and garlic in a bowl.
3. Toss the chicken in the sauce and place in the foil lined baking sheet.
4. Cook for 30 minutes, turning halfway through.
5. Drizzle with the remaining honey and serve.

Lemon Chicken & Asparagus

Servings: 4

Ingredients:

- 4 boneless, skinless chicken breasts
- 2 tbsp butter
- Lemon pepper, to taste
- 1/2 cup lemon juice
- 2 cups chopped asparagus

Directions:

1. Pound the chicken breasts out to 1/4" thickness. Pat the chicken dry.
2. Melt the butter in a skillet over medium heat.
3. Add the chicken and cook for 5 minutes on each side. Sprinkle each side with lemon pepper. Transfer to a plate once it is cooked.
4. Add the chopped asparagus to the same pan and sauté until bright green. Pour the lemon juice over the asparagus and cook for another minute or two. Remove from pan and serve with chicken.

Barbecue Chicken Bake

Servings: 4-6

Ingredients:

- 4 boneless, skinless chicken breasts
- 1 16-oz can of refrigerated biscuits
- 1 18-oz bottle of barbecue sauce
- 2 cups shredded mozzarella cheese

Directions:

1. Preheat your oven to 350 degrees F and spray a 9x13-inch casserole dish with nonstick spray.
2. Cut the chicken breasts into 1-inch pieces.
3. Cook the chicken in a medium skillet over medium-high heat. Cook until done.
4. Cut each biscuit into 8 pieces and set aside.
5. Pour the barbecue sauce over the chicken and stir to combine.
6. Add the biscuit pieces to the chicken and gently stir to combine.
7. Spread the mixture evenly into the prepared casserole dish. Sprinkle cheese on top.
8. Bake for 30 minutes then serve.

Broccoli Chicken Casserole

Servings: 4

Ingredients:

- 3 cups cooked shredded chicken
- 4 cups cooked rice
- 16 oz chopped broccoli florets
- 1 can cream of mushroom soup
- 1 cup shredded cheddar cheese

Directions:

1. Preheat your oven to 350 degrees F.
2. Mix all of the ingredients into a bowl then pour into a 9x13-inch baking dish.
3. Bake for 30 minutes then serve.

Crispy Ranch Chicken

Servings: 6

Ingredients:

- 6 skinless, boneless chicken breasts
- 1 cup ranch dressing
- 1 1/2 cups bread crumbs
- 1 1/2 cups crushed corn flakes

Directions:

1. Preheat your oven to 375 degrees F and spray a baking dish with nonstick spray.
2. Pour the ranch dressing into a shallow bowl.
3. Pour the bread crumbs and crushed corn flakes into a separate shallow bowl. Stir together well.
4. Dip the chicken breasts into the ranch and coat each side.
5. Dip the chicken breasts into the crumb mixture and coat well.
6. Place into the prepared dish and bake for 35-45 minutes or until crispy.

Barbeque Chicken Sweet Potatoes

Servings: 2

Ingredients:

- 2 medium sweet potatoes
- 1 lb boneless, skinless chicken breasts
- 1/2 cup barbeque sauce

Directions:

1. Cook and shred the chicken breasts.
2. Preheat your oven to 425 degrees F.
3. Cut the sweet potatoes in half.
4. Lay sweet potatoes, cut side up, on a large baking sheet and roast until tender. It should take about 35-40 minutes.
5. In a saucepan over medium heat, stir together the shredded chicken and barbeque sauce until warm.
6. Top each potato with scoops of chicken and spoon additional barbeque sauce over each potato.

BEEF RECIPES

Grilled Skirt Steak with Corn Salsa

Servings: 4

Ingredients:

- 2 lbs skirt steak
- 2 ears corn, husked
- 1 large poblano chile
- Olive oil

Directions:

1. Light a grill or preheat your oven to 425 degrees F.
2. Rub the corn and the chile with oil and grill over high heat until the corn is lightly browned and the chile is lightly charred, about 3-4 minutes.
3. Peel, core, and dice the poblano. Cut the kernels from the corn cobs.
4. Place half of the poblano and corn to a blender with 2 tbsp of olive oil and 2 tbsp of water and puree.
5. In a small bowl, toss together the remaining poblano and corn kernels with 2 tbsp oil.
6. Rub the steaks with oil and grill over high heat for about 6 minutes, turning over once.
7. Place the steak on a plate and let it rest for 5 minutes then slice into thin strips.
8. Spoon the salsa and the poblano corn mixture over the steak for serving.

Meatloaf

Servings: 6

Ingredients:

- 1.5 lbs hamburger meat
- 1 box Kraft Stove-Top Stuffing mix
- 1/2 cup milk
- 1 cup ketchup

Directions:

1. Preheat your oven to 350 degrees F.
2. Add all three ingredients into a large mixing bowl and mix together well.
3. Place the mixture into a baking dish and cover with foil.
4. Bake for one hour then serve.

Tangy Slow Cooker Meatball Subs

Servings: 10

Ingredients:

- 28 oz frozen precooked meatballs
- 18-oz jar of grape jelly
- 12-oz jar of chili sauce
- 10 sub sandwich rolls

Directions:

1. Add all of the ingredients to your slow cooker and cook on low for 4 hours.
2. Toast the rolls if desired and spoon the meatballs with sauce over the open rolls.

Crescent Taco Bake

Servings: 8

Ingredients:

- 2 lbs ground beef
- 2 packets of taco seasoning
- 2 cans rotel tomatoes
- 2 cups shredded cheddar cheese
- 2 cans refrigerated crescent rolls

Directions:

1. Preheat your oven to 375 degrees F.
2. Brown the ground beef and drain off the fat.
3. Return the meat to the skillet and stir in the taco seasoning and the rotel tomatoes (and juice). Mix well and simmer for 5-7 minutes.
4. Spray a 9x13-inch casserole dish with non-stick spray.
5. Unroll one can of crescent rolls and press the rolls into the pan.
6. Top the rolls with the ground beef mixture.
7. Top with shredded cheddar cheese.
8. Unroll the other can of crescent rolls and top the beef/cheese with the rolls.
9. Bake for 25 minutes.

Slow Cooker Beef Stroganoff

Servings: 4

Ingredients:

- 1 lb beef stew meat
- 1 packet Lipton dry onion soup mix
- 23 oz can condensed cream of mushroom soup
- 8 oz egg noodles
- 8 oz cream cheese, softened

Directions:

1. Stir the stew meat, onion soup mix, and cream of mushroom soup mixture into your slow cooker and stir together.
2. Cook on low for 3-4 hours.
3. Stir the softened cream cheese into the beef mixture, cover and let cook for another hour.
4. Prepare the egg noodles according to package directions.
5. Serve the beef mixture over the noodles.

Baked Ravioli with Spinach

Servings: 4

Ingredients:

- 2 cups tomato sauce
- 1 20-oz package refrigerated spinach and mozzarella ravioli
- 2 cups shredded mozzarella cheese
- 3 cups baby spinach
- 1/4 cup grated parmesan cheese

Directions:

1. Preheat your oven to 350 degrees F and spray a 9x9-inch casserole dish with nonstick spray.
2. Pour 1 cup of tomato sauce into the bottom of the prepared dish. Place a layer of half of the ravioli, then a layer of spinach, a layer of mozzarella cheese, then repeat layers.
3. Bake uncovered for 30 minutes.
4. Top with parmesan cheese before serving.

Slow Cooker Beef and Gravy

Servings: 4

Ingredients:

- 2 lbs sirloin steak, cut into strips
- 1 package onion soup mix
- 1/4 cup water
- 1 can golden mushroom soup

Directions:

1. Place the onion soup mix, water, and mushroom soup mix into your slow cooker and stir together.
2. Place the steak into your slow cooker and stir.
3. Cook on low for 6 hours.

Sloppy Joe Casserole

Servings: 6

Ingredients:

- 2 1/2 lbs lean ground beef
- 2 cans of Manwich sloppy joe mix
- 1 roll of refrigerator crescent rolls
- 2 cups shredded mozzarella

Directions:

1. Preheat your oven to 350 degrees F and spray a 9x13 baking dish with cooking spray.
2. Brown the ground beef in a large skillet over medium high heat. Drain off any grease.
3. Add both cans of Manwich to the cooked meat. Bring to a steady simmer then reduce heat to low.
4. Unroll the package of crescent rolls and lay them out on the bottom of the baking dish.
5. Sprinkle half of the cheese onto the crescent rolls.
6. Pour the Manwich meat mixture over the cheese.
7. Top the meat mixture with the rest of the cheese.
8. Bake for 20-25 minutes.

Meatball Sliders

Makes 24 sliders

Ingredients:

- 1 28 oz bag of frozen precooked meatballs
- 1 18-oz jar grape jelly
- 1 12-oz jar chili sauce
- 24 rolls or slider buns
- 24 slices of cheese

Directions:

1. In your slow cooker, stir together the grape jelly and chili sauce.
2. Add the frozen meatballs to the mixture in your slow cooker and stir.
3. Cook on high for 3 hours or on low for 6 hours.
4. Serve on slider buns topped with cheese.

Philly Cheesesteaks

Servings: 4

Ingredients:

- 4 hoagie rolls
- 2 lbs sirloin steak, thinly sliced
- 1 white onion, thinly sliced
- 1 bell pepper, thinly sliced
- 8 slices provolone cheese

Directions:

1. Preheat your oven to 400 degrees F.
2. Spray a large skillet with cooking spray and heat to medium-high.
3. Season the sliced steak with salt and pepper and cook until cooked through.
4. Add in the onions and peppers and cook until the onions are translucent.
5. Slice the hoagie rolls long ways down the center.
6. Place 2 slices of cheese on one side of each roll.
7. Top the other side of each roll with steak, peppers, and onions.
8. Place the open rolls in the oven for 3-5 minutes or until the cheese is melted.

Beef Macaroni and Cheese

Servings: 8

Ingredients:

- 1 onion, diced
- 1 28-oz can crushed tomatoes
- 2 lbs ground beef
- 1 box macaroni noodles
- 2 cups shredded cheddar cheese

Directions:

1. Preheat your oven to 400 degrees F and spray a 9x13 baking dish with cooking spray.
2. Brown the ground beef with the onion in a large skillet over medium-high heat.
3. Add the crushed tomatoes to the browned beef. Stir well and bring to a simmer. Reduce heat to low.
4. Cook the macaroni in boiling water for half of the time the directions say. Drain well.
5. Stir the noodles into the ground beef mixture. Stir half of the cheddar cheese.
6. Transfer the mixture to the prepared baking dish.
7. Top with the remaining cheese.
8. Bake for 30-35 minutes or until bubbly.

Beef Brisket

Servings: 8

Ingredients:

- 3 lbs beef brisket
- 1 cup barbeque sauce
- 1/3 cup soy sauce
- 1 cup water

Directions:

1. Preheat your oven to 300 degrees F.
2. In a small bowl, whisk together the sauces and water.
3. Place a very large sheet of foil in a large roasting pan.
4. Place the brisket on the foil and pour the sauce over it.
5. Wrap the brisket in the foil.
6. Roast for 3 hours (1 hour per lb of meat).
7. Remove from the oven and let it rest, still covered with foil, for 20 minutes.

Slow Cooker Beef Fajitas

Servings: 6

Ingredients:

- 1 onion, cut into slices
- 2 bell peppers, sliced
- 2 lbs thinly sliced beef, cut into strips
- 1 package fajita seasoning
- 1 cup beef broth

Directions:

1. Place the onions, peppers, and beef into your slow cooker.
2. Sprinkle the fajita seasoning over the mixture.
3. Cook on high for 5 hours or on low for 8 hours.

Slow Cooker Beef Burritos

Makes 8

Ingredients:

- 2 lbs beef stew meat
- 28-oz can enchilada sauce
- 1 beef bullion
- 8 burrito size flour tortillas
- 2 cups shredded cheese

Directions:

1. Place beef, enchilada sauce, and beef bouillon in the slow cooker and cook on low for 7-8 hours.
2. Shred the beef with a fork.
3. Spoon beef mixture onto each tortilla, add a couple tbsp of cheese to each, and roll up.
4. Place each burrito in a baking dish and broil for 3-4 minutes.

Meatball Casserole

Servings: 6

Ingredients:

- 1 28 oz bag of frozen precooked meatballs
- 1 45-oz jar of pasta sauce
- 2 cups shredded mozzarella cheese
- 1 cup shredded parmesan cheese
- Italian seasoning, to taste

Directions:

1. Preheat your oven to 350 degrees F.
2. Spread some pasta sauce into the bottom of a 9x13 inch casserole dish.
3. Arrange the meatballs on top of the pasta sauce.
4. Pour more sauce over the meatballs.
5. Sprinkle the cheeses on top of the sauce.
6. Sprinkle the cheese with Italian seasoning.
7. Bake for 20-25 minutes or until bubbly.

Ravioli Casserole

Servings: 6

Ingredients:

- 1 lb ground beef
- 1 28-oz jar spaghetti sauce
- 1 25-oz package frozen cheese ravioli
- 2 cups shredded mozzarella cheese

Directions:

1. In a large skillet, brown the ground beef then drain.
2. Preheat your oven to 400 degrees F.
3. Pour 1/3 of the spaghetti sauce into the bottom of a 9x9-inch casserole dish.
4. Top the sauce with half the ravioli, half the beef, and 1/2 cup of cheese. Repeat the layers.
5. Top with the remaining sauce and cheese.
6. Cover and bake for 40 minutes or until bubbly.

Ranch Roast Beef Sandwiches

Servings: 6

Ingredients:

- 2 lb boneless chuck roast
- 1 packet ranch seasoning
- 1 tsp garlic salt
- 6 French rolls
- 6 slices mozzarella cheese

Directions:

1. Place the chuck roast, ranch seasoning, and garlic salt in your slow cooker and cook for 8 hours on low.
2. Shred the beef with 2 forks and serve on French rolls topped with mozzarella cheese.

Slow Cooker Steak Stuffing

Servings: 6

Ingredients:

- 2 lbs sirloin steak
- 1 box cornbread stuffing mix
- 1 can rotel tomatoes
- 1/2 stick butter, melted

Directions:

1. Place the steak into your slow cooker.
2. In a medium bowl, stir together the stuffing, tomatoes, and butter
3. Pour the stuffing mixture over the steak in the slow cooker.

Cook on low for 8 hours or on high for 4 hours.

PORK RECIPES

Maple Slow Cooker Ham

Servings: 6

Ingredients:

- 4 lb precooked boneless ham
- 1 cup maple syrup
- 1/2 cup brown sugar
- 3 tbsp Dijon honey mustard

Directions:

1. Place the ham in your slow cooker.
2. In a small bowl, mix together the maple syrup, brown sugar, and honey mustard.
3. Pour the mixture over the ham.
4. Cover and cook on low for 4 hours.

Cajun Alfredo

Servings: 4

Ingredients:

- 1 lb smoked sausage, cut into 1/4-inch slices
- 8 oz fettucine or pasta of your choice
- 2 cups heavy cream
- 1 tbsp Cajun seasoning
- 1 cup grated parmesan cheese

Directions:

1. Prepare pasta according to package directions to al dente. Drain and set aside.
2. Sauté the sausage over medium high heat in a large skillet for 6-8 minutes.
3. Add in the cream and Cajun seasoning. Reduce heat to medium-low and gently simmer while stirring for 4-5 minutes or until thick.
4. Remove from heat and stir in the parmesan cheese.
5. Add in the pasta and toss to coat.

Bacon Asparagus Pasta

Servings: 4

Ingredients:

- 1/2 lb linguine
- 8 strips of bacon, diced
- 8 oz asparagus, trimmed and chopped
- 1/2 cup dry white wine
- 1 cup grated parmesan cheese

Directions:

1. Cook the pasta according to package directions to al dente.
2. Cook the bacon in a medium saucepan until crispy. Remove from the pan with a slotted spoon and set aside.
3. Add asparagus to the bacon grease and sauté for 5-6 minutes. Remove from the pan with a slotted spoon and set aside.
4. Add the white wine to the pan and scrape the bottom of the pan. Continue cooking for 5 minutes.
5. When the pasta is cooked, drain it and add the pasta, asparagus, bacon, and half of the cheese to the sauté pan and gently stir until combined.
6. Sprinkle the top with the remaining cheese and serve.

Mini Tortilla Pizzas

Servings: 4

Ingredients:

- 3 8-inch flour tortillas
- 1 cup pizza sauce
- 1 cup shredded mozzarella cheese
- 1/3 cup grated parmesan cheese
- 48 mini pepperonis

Directions:

1. Preheat your oven to 425 degrees F and lightly spray a muffin tin with nonstick spray.
2. Lay the tortillas on a flat surface, and using an empty can or biscuit cutter, cut 4 medium circles out of each tortilla.
3. Place one tortilla circle into the bottom of each muffin tin. Press it down carefully.
4. Spread 1 tbsp of pizza sauce into each muffin tin.
5. Sprinkle the sauce with mozzarella and parmesan.
6. Top the cheese with pepperonis.
7. Place the muffin tin into the oven and bake for 12 minutes then serve.

Dijon Roasted Pork Loin

Servings: 4

Ingredients:

- 1-lb pork tenderloin
- 2 tbsp Dijon mustard
- 2 tbsp honey
- 1 onion, thinly sliced

Directions:

1. Preheat your oven to 400 degrees F.
2. Spray a 9x9-inch baking dish with nonstick spray.
3. Place the onion slices in the bottom of the prepared dish.
4. Place the pork loin on top of the onions.
5. Stir together the Dijon mustard and honey.
6. Brush half of the mustard mixture over the pork.
7. Cover with foil and bake for 30 minutes.
8. Remove from the oven and brush on the remaining sauce.
9. Broil for 5 minutes.
10. Let the pork rest on the counter for 10 minutes before slicing.

Stromboli

Servings: 6

Ingredients:

- 1 11-oz can of refrigerated thin crust pizza dough
- 1/2 cup pizza sauce, plus extra for dipping
- 2-3 oz of sliced pepperoni
- 2 cups mozzarella cheese

Directions:

1. Preheat your oven to 400 degrees F.
2. Line a large baking sheet with parchment paper.
3. Stretch the pizza crust out onto the parchment paper.
4. Top the crust with sauce, cheese, and pepperonis.
5. Starting on one side, carefully roll the dough up into a roll.
6. Place in the center of the parchment paper, seam side down.
7. Cut several diagonal slits into the crust.
8. Bake for 20 minutes or until golden brown.
9. Serve with extra marinara for dipping.

Teriyaki Pork Loin

Servings: 6

Ingredients:

- 1 cup teriyaki sauce
- 2 tbsp brown sugar
- 1 garlic clove, minced
- 2 lb pork loin

Directions:

1. Whisk together the sauce, brown sugar, and garlic.
2. Place the pork loin in a large shallow dish.
3. Pour the sauce over the pork loin.
4. Cover and refrigerate for several hours.
5. Preheat oven to 400 degrees.
6. Place pork loin in a baking dish and cook for 20-30 minutes.

Pepperoni Roll-Ups

Servings: 8

Ingredients:

- 1 can crescent rolls
- 40 slices of pepperoni
- 4 pieces of mozzarella string cheese, cut in half
- Garlic powder
- Marinara sauce

Directions:

1. Preheat your oven to 375 degrees F.
2. Unroll the crescent rolls and separate them into 8 triangles.
3. Place 5 pepperonis and one string cheese half on the large end of the crescent roll.
4. Roll up the crescent rolls and sprinkle each of them with garlic powder.
5. Place the rolls on a greased baking sheet and bake for 12-15 minutes, or until golden brown.
6. Serve with warm marinara sauce.

Slow Cooker Pulled Pork

Servings: 4

Ingredients:

- 2 lbs pork tenderloin
- 1 can root beer
- 18-oz bottle of barbeque sauce

Directions:

1. Place the tenderloin in the slow cooker and pour the can of root beer over it.
2. Cook on low for 6 hours or until the pork shreds easily.
3. Drain off most of the root beer and shred pork completely with a fork.
4. Pour the barbeque sauce over the pork and stir.
5. Cook on low for another hour or two before serving.

Slow Cooker Honey Mustard Pork Chops

Servings: 6

Ingredients:

- 1 1/2 lbs boneless pork chops
- 1 onion, sliced
- 3 tbsp honey
- 3 tbsp Dijon mustard

Directions:

1. Place the pork chops and onions in your slow cooker.
2. In a small bowl, stir together the honey, mustard, and pepper.
3. Pour the honey mustard mixture over the pork chops.
4. Cook on low for 4 hours or on high for 8 hours.

Slow Cooker Fiesta Pork Chops

Servings: 6

Ingredients:

- 6 pork chops
- 1 can chili beans in chili sauce
- 2 cups salsa
- 1 cup corn
- 1 small can green chiles

Directions:

1. Place the pork chops into your slow cooker.
2. In a small bowl, stir together the rest of the ingredients.
3. Pour the mixture over the pork chops.
4. Cook on low for 6 hours.

Slow Cooker Ham

Servings: 6

Ingredients:

- 1 precooked spiral cut ham
- 1 cup brown sugar
- 1 can pineapple rings
- 15 maraschino cherries

Directions:

1. Sprinkle half of the brown sugar into the bottom of a slow cooker.
2. Place the ham on top of the brown sugar and pour the pineapple rings and juice on top.
3. Place the cherries over the ham.
4. Sprinkle the rest of the brown sugar on top of the ham.
5. Cook for 4-6 hours on low.

Slow Cooker Barbeque Pork Ribs

Servings: 4

Ingredients:

- 2.5 lb rack of baby back pork ribs
- 1 tbsp brown sugar
- Salt and pepper
- 1 1/2 cups barbeque sauce

Directions:

1. Season the ribs with salt, pepper, and brown sugar.
2. Place the rack of ribs in your slow cooker with the more meaty side facing the wall of the slow cooker. You will have to bend it and wrap it around the inside.
3. Pour barbeque sauce over the ribs.

Cook on low for 8 hours.

FISH RECIPES

Thai Baked Salmon

Servings: 6

Ingredients:

- 6 6-oz salmon filets
- Salt, to taste
- 1/2 cup plus 2 tbsp sweet chile sauce
- 3 tbsp chopped green onions

Directions:

1. Place the salmon filets in a large baking dish and sprinkle with salt.
2. Top the filets with 1/2 cup sweet chile sauce. Cover and marinate in the refrigerator for at least 2 hours.
3. Turn the oven broiler on high and line a baking sheet with foil. Spray the foil with cooking spray.
4. Place the filets on the prepared baking sheet and coat with the remaining marinade.
5. Broil for 8 minutes, rotating the baking sheet once.
6. Remove from the oven and drizzle with the 2 tbsp of chile sauce.
7. Broil for another 5 minutes.
8. Sprinkle with chopped green onions and serve.

Slow Cooker Garlic Tilapia

Servings: 4

Ingredients:

- 4 tilapia filets
- 2 tbsp butter
- 1 tbsp minced garlic
- Salt and pepper, to taste

Directions:

1. Place the tilapia filets on a large sheet of aluminum foil.
2. Generously season each filet with salt and pepper.
3. Divide the butter and garlic between the four filets and top each of them.
4. Wrap the foil around the fish, sealing it as tightly as possible.

Place in your slow cooker and cook on high for 2 hours.

MEATLESS RECIPES

Avocado Egg Chilaquiles

Servings: 4

Ingredients:

- 1 16-oz jar salsa verde
- 1 large avocado, peeled and pit removed
- 8 cups broken tortilla chips
- 1 cup grated Monterey Jack cheese
- 4 large eggs, fried over medium (or however you like them cooked)

Directions:

1. Heat a large saucepan over medium-high heat.
2. Place the salsa and the avocado in a blender and blend until smooth.
3. Pour the avocado/sauce mixture into the heated pan.
4. Add the tortillas to the saucepan and toss to coat.
5. Divide the mixture to 4 plates. Top with cheese and 1 egg per plate.

Butternut Squash Panini

Servings: 4

Ingredients:

- 1 medium butternut squash, peeled and sliced into 1/4 inch slices
- 1 tbsp olive oil + more for brushing
- 8-oz fresh mozzarella, drained and sliced
- 8 slices of thick whole wheat bread

Directions:

1. Preheat your oven to 400 degrees F.
2. Brush the slices of butternut squash with olive oil and place them on a rimmed baking sheet. Bake them for 40-45 minutes or until tender and beginning to brown around the edges. Turn them over halfway through cooking.
3. Preheat Panini press* to medium-high heat.
4. Brush one side of each slice of bread with olive oil.
5. Divide the squash and mozzarella evenly onto the non-oiled side of 4 slices of bread.
6. Top with the remaining slices of bread and grill until golden brown, 6-8 minutes.

*If you don't have a Panini press, you can use a sandwich press or a waffle iron!

Caprese Naan Pizza

Servings: 2

Ingredients:

- 1/4 cup balsamic vinegar
- 2 pieces of naan
- 1/2 cup cherry or grape tomatoes, halved
- 1/2 cup small fresh mozzarella balls
- 1/4 cup fresh basil, chopped thin

Directions:

1. Heat the balsamic vinegar in a saucepan over medium heat. Simmer and let it thicken for 8-10.
2. Heat a grill pan over medium-high heat. Spray both sides of on piece of naan with cooking spray and press it into the heated pan with a spatula. Cook on each side for 2-3 minutes until grill pan lines appear. Repeat with the other piece of naan.
3. Top each piece of naan with tomatoes, cheese, and basil.
4. Drizzle with the thickened balsamic and serve.

Parmesan Spinach Pasta

Servings: 4

Ingredients:

- 8 oz thin spaghetti
- 3 tbsp butter
- 2 cloves garlic, minced
- 6 cups baby spinach
- 1 cup grated parmesan cheese

Directions:

1. Cook the pasta according to package directions to al dente. Drain the pasta but save 1/2 cup of the pasta water. Set pasta aside.
2. Melt the butter in a large pot over medium heat. Sauté the garlic for 2 minutes.
3. Add in the pasta and spinach. Cook and toss until spinach leaves are wilted. If pasta starts to dry out, add in some of the reserved pasta water.
4. Stir in 1/2 cup of parmesan cheese.
5. Serve topped with additional cheese.

Greek Tarts

Servings: 2

Ingredients:

- 2 large, thick slices of sourdough bread
- 1/4 cup hummus
- 6 artichoke hearts, cut in half length-wise
- 10 pieces of sundried tomato
- 2 tbsp crumbled feta cheese

Directions:

1. Preheat your oven to 450 degrees F.
2. Spread each slice of bread with hummus.
3. Top each slice with artichoke hearts, sundried tomatoes, and feta.
4. Set each slice of bread on a baking sheet and bake until crisp, 4-6 minutes.

Spaghetti with Spinach Sauce

Servings: 4

Ingredients:

- 2 tbsp olive oil
- 3 cloves garlic, minced
- 1 16-oz bag of fresh baby spinach
- 8 oz spaghetti noodles
- 1 cup grated parmesan cheese

Directions:

1. Heat the olive oil in a large saucepan over medium high heat.
2. Add the garlic and sauté for 2 minutes.
3. Add the spinach and sauté until wilted. Remove from heat and set aside.
4. Cook the pasta according to package directions and reserve a cup of the pasta water before draining. Set the pasta and reserved water aside.
5. Add the spinach and garlic to a food processor with the cheese and half of the pasta water. Blend until a smooth sauce forms. Add more pasta water if needed.
6. Add the pasta and the sauce to the pan over medium heat and stir until heated through then serve.

Kale Pasta Salad

Servings: 6

Ingredients:

- 1 lb garden rotini (or pasta of choice)
- 1 pint cherry or grape tomatoes
- 1 bunch kale; washed, stemmed, and chopped
- 1 16-oz bottle creamy Caesar dressing
- 4 oz grated parmesan cheese

Directions:

1. Cook the pasta according to package directions to al dente. Drain and place it in a large bowl.
2. Preheat your oven to 425 degrees F and roast the tomatoes on a baking sheet until they are soft and begin to burst, about 10 minutes.
3. Add the chopped kale and roasted tomatoes to the pasta.
4. Add half of the dressing to the pasta and stir well. Add more dressing if desired.
5. Sprinkle with parmesan cheese.
6. Refrigerate for an hour or longer before serving.

Broccoli Cheese Soup

Servings: 4

Ingredients:

- 2 cups vegetable stock
- 2 cups chopped broccoli florets
- 1 small onion, diced
- 1 15-oz can evaporated milk
- 2 cups shredded sharp cheddar cheese

Directions:

1. Stir together the vegetable stock, diced onion, and broccoli in a medium saucepan over medium heat until it comes to a boil.
2. Reduce heat to medium and boil for 5 minutes.
3. Stir in the evaporated milk and cook for another 5 minutes.
4. Remove from heat and stir in the cheese until melted.

Zucchini Boats

Servings: 4

Ingredients:

- 4 medium zucchinis
- 1 cup shredded mozzarella cheese
- 2 cups marinara sauce

Directions:

1. Preheat your oven to 425 degrees F.
2. Slice each zucchini in half lengthwise and carefully scoop out the seeds.
3. Sprinkle a little mozzarella into each zucchini boat, then top it with marinara sauce. Top each boat with mozzarella cheese.
4. Bake for 10 minutes or until marinara is bubbly.
5. Serve immediately.

Pesto Pizza

Servings: 4

Ingredients:

- 1 medium sized pizza crust
- 1 cup basil pesto
- 1 large tomato, sliced
- 1 cup shredded mozzarella cheese

Directions:

1. If not precooked, bake pizza crust according to package directions.
2. Preheat oven to 400 degrees F.
3. Spread the pesto over the crust.
4. Top the crust with cheese and tomatoes.
5. Cook for 6-8 minutes or until cheese is melted and crust is crispy.

Chickpea and Basil Fritatta

Servings: 2

Ingredients:

- 4 large eggs
- 1/2 cup grated parmesan cheese
- 1 14-oz can chickpeas, drained and rinsed
- 4 leaves basil, finely chopped

Directions:

1. Preheat your oven to 400 degrees F.
2. Spray an 8-inch spring form pan with non-stick spray.
3. Whisk together the eggs and the cheese.
4. Place the chickpeas into the spring form pan.
5. Pour the egg and cheese mixture over the chickpeas.
6. Scatter chopped basil leaves over the eggs.
7. Bake for 15 minutes or until the center is set.
8. Gently remove from the spring form pan and serve.

Egg Spaghetti Squash Boats

Servings: 2

Ingredients:

- 1 spaghetti squash
- 4 tbsp salsa, divided
- 1 avocado; peeled, pitted, and chopped
- 2 eggs
- 2 tbsp Sriracha, optional

Directions:

1. Preheat your oven to 400 degrees F. Line a baking sheet with parchment paper.
2. Cut spaghetti squash in half lengthwise and scoop out the seeds. Place cut side down on the prepared baking sheet and bake for 30 minutes. Remove from the oven and let it cool for 10-15 minutes or until its cool enough to handle.
3. Turn the oven up to 425 degrees F.
4. Using a fork, separate the squash strands inside the shells.
5. Add 2 tbsp of salsa to each half of the squash and gently stir into the strands.
6. Top each half with avocado slices.
7. Break an egg into each squash shell.
8. Place back into the oven and bake for 20 minutes or until the egg whites are set.
9. Drizzle with Sriracha, if desired, and serve.

Broccoli Quinoa Quesadillas

Servings: 4

Ingredients:

- 1/4 cup uncooked quinoa
- 1/2 cup chopped broccoli florets
- 1 cup shredded cheddar cheese
- 2 8 or 10-inch flour tortillas
- 2 tsp olive oil

Directions:

1. Cook the quinoa according to package directions.
2. Combine the quinoa, broccoli, and cheese in a medium bowl.
3. Divide mixture evenly onto one half of each tortilla. Fold tortilla in half, with the mixture on the inside.
4. Heat one tsp of oil in a medium skillet over medium heat.
5. Place 2 quesadillas in skillet and cook until browned, 2 or 3 minutes per side. Repeat with the remaining oil and quesadillas.

Sweet Potato and Asparagus Zoodles

Servings: 4

Ingredients:

- 2 small zucchini
- 1 bunch of asparagus, trimmed and chopped
- 2 sweet potatoes
- 1 cup cheddar cheese
- 1 cup heavy cream

Directions:

1. Preheat your oven to 350 degrees F.
2. Using a peeler, spiralizer, or mandolin, slice zucchini into pasta.
3. Peel and chop the sweet potato into cubes.
4. Place the asparagus and sweet potato on a baking sheet.
5. Roast in the preheated oven for 30-35 minutes or until potatoes are soft.
6. Spray a large saucepan with nonstick spray and add the cheese and cream. Stir until the cheese melts and cream becomes thick.
7. Remove from heat and add in the zucchini noodles and toss to coat.
8. Top with the roasted sweet potato and asparagus.

French Bread Pizza

Servings: 4

Ingredients:

- 1 loaf of French bread, halved lengthwise
- 1 cup pesto
- 2 cups shredded mozzarella cheese
- 1/2 cup sun-dried tomatoes

Directions:

1. Preheat your oven to 350 degrees F.
2. Place bread on a large baking sheet.
3. Top each half of the bread with pesto, 1 cup of cheese, and tomatoes.
4. Bake for 10-15 minutes or until cheese is melted and bread is crisp.

Baked Gnocchi with Ricotta

Servings: 4

Ingredients:

- 1 16-oz package gnocchi
- 1 cup marinara sauce
- 1 cup ricotta cheese
- 1/2 cup grated parmesan cheese
- Chopped parsley, for garnish

Directions:

1. Cook the gnocchi according to package directions and drain.
2. Preheat your oven to 400 degrees F.
3. Place the gnocchi in a 9x9-inch baking dish.
4. Pour the marinara over the gnocchi.
5. Dollop the ricotta over the marinara and then sprinkle with parmesan.
6. Cook for 10-15 minutes or until cheese is melted.
7. Top with parsley before serving.

Coconut Lime Quinoa

Servings: 2

Ingredients:

- 1 cup uncooked quinoa
- 1 13-oz can of coconut milk
- 1/4 cup water
- Salt, to taste
- Juice and zest from 1 lime

Directions:

1. Rinse quinoa in a fine mesh strainer.
2. Place quinoa, coconut milk, water, and salt into a saucepan over medium heat. Bring to a boil, reduce heat to low, cover, and simmer for 15-20 minutes or until the liquid has been absorbed.
3. Remove from the heat and let the quinoa set for 5 minutes.
4. Fluff the quinoa then stir in the lime zest and juice then serve.

Spinach Pesto Quinoa

Servings: 4

Ingredients:

- 2 cups uncooked quinoa
- 6 cups spinach, roughly chopped
- 4 tbsp pesto
- 1/2 tsp salt
- 1/2 cup parmesan cheese

Directions:

1. Cook the quinoa according to package directions.

2. Stir the spinach, pesto, salt, and parmesan cheese into the cooked quinoa over medium heat. Cook for 5 minutes or until the spinach is wilted.

Notes

Notes

Made in the USA
San Bernardino, CA
28 January 2017